Done With the Crying
WORKBOOK

FOR PARENTS OF ESTRANGED ADULT CHILDREN

Sheri McGregor

Sowing Creek Press

San Marcos, California

Sowing Creek Press
711 Center Drive, Ste. 105, Box 129
San Marcos, CA 92069
Email: info@sowingcreekpress.com
www.sowingcreekpress.com

Done With The Crying WORKBOOK: For Parents of Estranged Adult Children/Sheri McGregor. —1st ed.
ISBN: 978-0-9973522-4-5 (print)

DISCLAIMER:
Although care was taken to ensure the research and information in this book was correct at the time it went to press, the author and publisher do not assume and hereby disclaim any liability to any party for loss, damage, or disruption due to any errors or omissions—whether the result of negligence, accident, or any other cause. This book does not substitute for medical, spiritual, or psychological advice. Content is based on the author's personal experience, as well as studies and research, but is the author's opinion. Readers should contact a licensed physician, psychiatrist, psychologist, or other licensed practitioner for diagnosis and care.

Recommendations for
Done With the Crying

HELP AND HEALING FOR MOTHERS
OF ESTRANGED ADULT CHILDREN

Done With the Crying was the first book I found when my estrangement started and it was a lifeline for me! I kept the book beside my bed and read and worked on the exercises daily. I still look at my highlighted pages and exercise answers to this day. I know without a doubt that this book helped me survive the horrible first 6 months of the estrangement. I would not have made it without the help, encouragement and resources that this book offered me. I am a practicing Family Practice doctor and none of my training in psychiatry or medical textbooks helped me through the healing process, but *Done With the Crying* did! I now recommend this book as first-line treatment for any of my patients that encounter estrangement in their families. It is truly a lifeline of everything you need to start getting your life back after estrangement hits you.

—Dr. Alison Garza, M.D., Board Certified Family Practice

The book is a must read for parents of estranged adult children and mental health professionals working with these families. Sheri McGregor's work is a breath of fresh air offering a new perspective and providing support, encouragement, resources, and compassion to good parents who have found themselves in an unimaginable situation.

—Maritza Parks, LMHC, *Inspired Journeys Counseling*

Done With The Crying is for any (and all) family member who wants to heal and move forward. This wonderful book will help you see how you can hold your chin up high, dry your eyes, and get on with your life.

—Joi Sigers, *Self Help Dailly.com*

Done With the Crying also provides much time for reflection, for taking time to think about ones life and to read the stories of other women who are going through a similar situation. The book is easy to read, and provides much support and insight in a gentle and understanding way.

—Hennie Weiss, M.A., *Metapsychology Online Reviews*

This is my best resource to assist families whose adult children have rejected them. In my role as a family life educator, I work with those affected by a loved one's mental illness, and the sad phenomenon of estrangement is rampant. I've searched for resources and education, but there is precious little available to help rejected parents move forward. It did not take me many pages in to see the value for my work, and often recommend this compassionately written book to parents and families who are in so much pain.

—Mara J. Briere, MA CFLE, President and Founder,
Grow a Strong Family, Inc.

Contents

A Message *from* Sheri McGregor

Dear Readers,

Here's the Workbook you've been asking for!

The *Done With the Crying Workbook for Parents of Estranged Adult Children* is intended as a supplement to the original book (*Done With The Crying: Help and Healing for Mothers of Estranged Adult Children*). It's not a replacement. I recommend reading or listening to the original book first. Its resources and information, as well additional scenarios, my story, and the examples of many anguished parents best supports your growth and recovery.

The Workbook exercises are nearly identical to those in the paperback version of the original book, but the larger page size provides additional writing space. Each activity is grouped under the chapter numbers where they originally appear, too. So, you can easily stop the audio or close the e-book at exercise prompts, and then turn to the Workbook. The exercises provide deeper insights and make the concepts in *Done With The Crying* personal to you and your unique set of circumstances. So, whether you're listening, using the e-book, or are doing the exercises again—as many readers say they do—this Workbook is for you.

Workbook users will be better oriented if they read the original book first, as well as better prepared to complete the exercises. Having said that, there are no set rules. *You're in charge—of your life, your happiness, and how you move forward.*

CHAPTER ONE

The Early Daze

Your world tilted, your adult child moved on, and you were left standing in the storm. Bewilderment, confusion, and a range of other emotions and behaviors is normal. There is science to explain your responses—and this chapter covers them.

✈ Give Voice to Your Experience

How we describe our pain can provide insights into its expression in our lives, thus help us move forward in productive ways. Some use visceral terms. Their hearts break, their legs grow weak, or they feel numb. Others call it a battle. They're under attack. Some focus on loss—of their child, their hope, and their identity. Many express fears or anxiety. Let's look at a few examples, and discover insights.

- *"I'm always on edge. Just one step away from falling."*
  Imagine being always "on edge." Anxiety rules this parent's life. Taken literally, she must guard against a compulsion to keep looking back, and moving toward the dangerous edge she describes. She may benefit from deep breathing and an ordered environment. Routines may help her take small but purposeful steps in another direction.

- *"I feel like I've been mauled by a bear."*
  How might the second parent take action? Should she just lie there, defeated? She may need to assess her situation, and admit how powerless she feels. She'll need to muster the strength to seek safe support that can help her heal from the emotional mauling.

- *"He might as well have stabbed me in the heart."*
  This parent expresses a devastating blow. Maybe her words provide insight into a need to care for her physical health. She may need to be extra wary of coping in physically harmful ways, and make efforts to take good care of herself. Perhaps her focus on her heart is significant. With a doctor's approval, routines to aid cardiovascular health are wise. The heart is also symbolic of the spirit, so watching for signs of depression, and facilitating joy might be helpful.

  Another woman said she felt as if her legs had been blown off, which provides a clue to her difficulty in moving forward. She may need support to get going again.

Now it's your turn. How do *you* describe the experience of estrangement? Write the first thought that comes to mind. If you feel up to it, write additional phrases to relay your pain, shock, and loss. Don't censor yourself. As you write, think of yourself as a loving friend and caring listener.

_____

_____

_____

_____

_____

_____

_____

_____

Read back what you've written—aloud if you can. Recent studies demonstrate that as we verbalize our emotions, the areas of the brain associated with language and speech become more active, while the areas associated with pain are less active.

Ancient storytellers who returned from a harrowing adventure or hunt, and then shared their tales beside the campfire, may have instinctively known that putting feelings into words was good for them. Among the parents I've interviewed, many expressed that they felt better by the end of the call. They echo the feelings of those who have shared their stories via the survey, in email, or in the forum. Put your feelings into words. It helps.

Read what you've written again. Just as we reflected on how the parents in the examples expressed anxiety, abandonment, or physical pain, contemplate your words. _What clues exist in your own words about how the experience of estrangement expresses itself in your life? What must you guard against?_

In the next set of lines, jot down thoughts about your own situation. _What can you do to help yourself?_

_____

_____

_____

_____

_____

_____

_____

✈ Observe, and Then Make a Plan

Consider your own experience with intrusive thoughts and memories. Can you make a plan to better handle those times as Julia did? Or perhaps you're more like Deanne. Answer the questions below.

- *What times of the day, week, or year are more difficult for you?*

_____

_____

_____

_____

_____

_____

_____

- *How can you change how you think about that time?*

_____

_____

_____

_____

_____

_____

_____

- *How can you use that time differently? Can you change your routine?*

_____

_____

_____

_____

_____

_____

_____

- *When might you practice mindfulness, even aside from thoughts about the estrangement? Jot down a few ideas. Refer back and follow through.*

_____

_____

_____

_____

_____

_____

_____

_____

✈ Know Your Feelings: Moving Ahead For Your Own Good

As you progress toward reclaiming your self-worth and happiness despite the estrangement, awareness can help. As you read the statements below, rate how you feel. Use a scale of one to five, with one meaning "don't agree," and five meaning "strongly agree." Write the number on the adjacent line. Wherever a pronoun was needed, I've used "he." Substitute what's appropriate in your situation.

— I have been hurting in this situation.
— My child can't mean what he says.
— It has been difficult to get over the pain.
— I have tried to make things right.
— If it wasn't for the spouse/partner/friend, my child wouldn't be doing this.
— I have done everything I can to mend the relationship.
— I can never let this go.
— It's not right for a mother to give up.
— In all honesty, I miss my child—but not the adult he became.
— After all I've done, my child shouldn't treat me like this.
— I can change how my child feels about our relationship.
— I cannot control my adult child's behavior.
— I do not miss the strife.
— My child doesn't mean to stay estranged.
— My child owes me respect and care.
— I have apologized for mistakes. I don't see what else I can do.
— My child is disrespectful, and does not honor his parents.
— I can only control myself.
— I'm tired of being angry.
— Whether I like it or not, my child has the right to keep me out of his life.
— I'm weary of self-censoring, and overthinking everything I say to try and keep the peace.
— It's difficult to accept estrangement without understanding it.
— I can sometimes control my child's behavior.
— If I'm honest, the relationship has not been satisfying.
— Despite the estrangement, I can give myself credit for my part in my adult child's success.
— I am determined to take action for my own well-being.
— I am not ready to accept this.
— My child needs to understand that this is a mistake.
— I am committed to moving forward in my life.
— I deserve to be happy.
— No matter what I have done, it has never been enough.
— I'm tired of tip-toeing around, trying not to set him off.

Now, look back and identify the statements you agree or disagree with the most. Paying close attention to those you've marked with a "5" (strongly agree) or a "1" (don't agree), a pattern may emerge. Maybe you're fed up and ready to get on with your own life. Or perhaps you believe your child is ungrateful, which prods your anger. Your beliefs about motherhood, unconditional love, and children's duty to honor parents may influence your emotions. Take note of where your feelings fall for each of the statements. Use the next set of lines to jot down a few thoughts about the exercise, your feelings about particular statements and what you've learned about your feelings.

_____

_____

_____

_____

_____

_____

_____

_____

_____

_____

_____

_____

Don't judge or criticize yourself. Mindfulness isn't about judging yourself or your feelings. Knowing where you stand in your determination to get on with your life right now provides a base point for future reference, and makes you aware of possible sticking points and areas where you might need to make more effort.

Healing requires acceptance of what you cannot change, recognition of what you must change, and a decision to take action. Read through the following statements, and consider how you feel about them.

The Pain
- I have been hurting in this situation.
- It has been difficult to get over the pain.

Acceptance
- I cannot control my adult child's behavior.
- I can only control myself.

Moving Forward
- I am determined to take action for my own well-being.
- I am committed to moving forward in my life.
- I deserve to be happy.

Most parents will readily agree with the first two statements. The reality of your grown son or daughter's rejection is painful, and getting over the pain can be a challenge. What about the "acceptance" statements? Can you accept that your child is in charge of his or her life? Accepting that you can only control your own actions is important if you're to let go of the pain.

For some, committing to the "moving forward" statements will elicit sadness or even guilt. But taking steps toward your own well-being does not have to mean you don't ever want to reconcile. Many of the parents reading this book will have already tried, maybe even repeatedly. Unable to do so, at least for the present, these parents recognize that they need to find a way to move forward—even while holding out hope they can reconnect in the future.

✈ *Notes*

_____

_____

_____

_____

_____

_____

_____

_____

_____

_____

_____

_____

_____

_____

_____

_____

✈ *Notes*

CHAPTER TWO

Why?

Cultural shifts, individual circumstances, nonsensical and non-existent reasons, as well as difficult truths may play a role in estrangements. All parents make mistakes. Reclaim a positive self-image and stop asking *why?* Learn to ask questions that help.

✈ Remember the Good You Did

Instead of sifting through memories for what went wrong, focus on the good you did. Did you protect your child? Feed him properly? Cheer her on? Support his interests? Entertain her friends? Show kindness?

Make a list. Write it down. Be to the point, or much more detailed. Your list is uniquely yours. Do the exercise the way it feels right for you. Some mothers won't want to look back at good memories in detail because it hurts them so much. If that's how you feel, keep this simple. Making a bulleted list of words or short phrases is fine. Others will find that giving equal time to looking back at all the good they did helps them let go of any mistakes they've been narrowing in on and blaming themselves for. *Do what's best for you.* Below are some helpful ideas.

Talk with someone supportive. A friend, your spouse, a relative, or your other children will know how involved you always were. Someone who was there as we did our best can help us remember all the good we did.

Look at old photographs or mementos. Items you've kept or photos of happy times can trigger memories of your active, positive role. For me, old photographs helped to validate my belief in myself. It was me who pointed the camera. I captured the grin on Dan's dirt-smudged face as he posed with his hand on the doorknob, ready to run back out to play. *I remember that moment.*

I was there when he posed with his siblings in the shade of a tree at a local botanical garden. It was me who photographed him monkeying around near the gorilla statues at the zoo. And I cooked the food that's arranged on our table in another photo where he sits with his fork in hand. The piles and piles of photographs provide an endless stream, proof of happy times.

I was there as he grew from boyhood innocence into an intelligent teenager, and a productive adult. I carted him and his friends to and from school events, rode along patiently as he first learned to drive, and watched with pride as he drove off alone in his very first car. Those memories are real. And no matter what, they are precious to me.

On paper, block out the stages of your child's life. You could tape several sheets of paper together, or put pages in a notebook. Use a page for each of several stages: babyhood, toddler years, elementary school ages. . . . Or focus on categories: sports, school, friends. . . . Using stages or interests may provide direction. In each section, jot down notes about the good you did. If it feels right to you, add pictures. Or use less than a full page, and write short phrases only.

Remember the point. I shed a few tears revisiting my memories, but renewed my self-image as a loving, attentive mother. From even before he was born, I cared for my son. I helped him grow. We did have fun together. Writing down the positive things you did as a parent helps reinforce them, and provides a list you can look at later.

Remember, *how* you do this exercise is up to you—make it as complex and detailed as you like. You could make a slide show, a scrapbook, or a collage of the field trips you drove for, parties you hosted, sports games you cheered at. . . . Or simply jot a short list to represent your role as a responsible, caring parent. If it's best for you, simply stroll through the years in your mind, and relive the successful moments in your memories. Remember the point: *Focus on the good you did.*

✈ Power-up a Positive Outlook: Three Steps

In Chapter One, we explored the idea of coping mindfully. Here, we build on the concept by gaining even more awareness of our thoughts and speech. Then we'll work on reshaping them. This exercise should be completed over a week or more. And it's a good technique to revisit whenever you find yourself feeling down in the dumps.

STEP ONE: Gain Awareness. If you became lost while driving, you could go in circles until you ran out of gas, and still be lost. However, if while driving you take stock of your surroundings then admit you're lost, you can stop, get directions or pull out a map, and alter your course. It's the same with the things we tell ourselves.

One day when I was feeling particularly low, and being vocal about it, my words hung in the air like a curse to predict my future: *I'll never get over this.*

What words do *you* say that form your outlook? What thoughts run through your mind to convince you you'll never be happy again? When we're hurting, we can get so caught up in our pain that negative, unhelpful thinking and speech become a habit. Let's change that now. For the next few days, make a practice of listening to yourself—your thoughts and your speech—so you can later redirect.

Write down any negative, complaining, self-pitying, hopeless words and phrases you hear coming out of your mouth or looping through your mind. Watch out for dark cloud dictates. *I'll never get over this. My heart will always be broken.* Listen for statements that set conditions on happiness, or otherwise limit you. *I just can't go on until this is resolved. I'm too old to start over now.* Recognize self-pity. *I never expected such hurt from my own child.* Maybe you convince yourself you're all alone: *Nobody understands.* Or ask yourself defeatist questions. *What's the point?*

These thoughts may represent the depth of your pain, but they're not helpful. And they can multiply. If you indulge in negative thoughts, statements, or questions, the mind easily builds upon them. *My son isn't the first person to betray me. Why do people always leave me?* Or maybe your negative thinking gets more generalized: *Bad things always happen to me.*

This sort of thinking, sometimes called "ruminating," prompts more of the same. Looping thoughts that make you feel worse and worse. Soon, you're shuffling along a deepening groove, burrowing into a cavern of despair. *Nobody understands. I might as well just hole up and never make new friends or see my old ones. If I try to socialize, I'll have to pretend. If I tell them what's happened to me, I'll only be judged, shamed and hurt more. Face it. I don't fit anymore. Not anywhere. Not ever again.*

At one point after my son's estrangement, I had to admit how far I'd sunk. I was concentrating on the loss, and consumed with worry about what else would go wrong and who would leave me. Usually optimistic, I was drowning myself in sorrow. You may find yourself at that point. I had to take control, and I know you can take control, too.

Clinical studies have linked these sorts of churning thoughts, rumination, to high blood pressure and to unhealthy behaviors such as binge drinking and overeating. Steer clear. Negative thinking and its consequences will only complicate matters.

When you catch yourself thinking negatively, notice your body too. Are you holding your breath? Clenching your jaw? Tightening your fists? Reaching for junk food or an extra glass of wine? You may be experiencing a harmful stress response. Changing your thoughts changes your body's responses too. Try focusing on anything you handled well, or imagine offering forgiveness. The way we think about things can reduce physical stress responses, and more positively affect our health.

To benefit from awareness, keep writing down the negativity that runs through your head. Jot down phrases that linger, and take notes about how they lead to other negative thoughts. If you then connect that sort of thinking to the events of your day, you may clearly see how they influence you, your interaction with others, and your overall mood.

Don't try to rush past this step. For some of you, the negativity may immediately spring to mind. But spend a few days listening to your thoughts and speech to make sure you're fully identifying it.

It's important to take your time, to really listen in on your thoughts, and to seriously contemplate how your outlook affects you.

_____

_____

_____

_____

_____

_____

_____

_____

_____

Review your notes. Based on what you've recorded in writing, create a list of negative adjectives to describe your emotional state. In the table below, leave the right-hand column blank for now. Use the left-hand column to write your descriptive words. A few from my list were: *sad, preoccupied, stuck, vulnerable,* and *pitiful.* Once you have your list, consider whether the words describe the *real* you. Is this how you were *before* the estrangement? Is the list representative of who you want to be?

Negative	Positive

Return to your notes for any repeated phrases or thoughts. *I'll never get over this. How could he do this to me? It must be my fault. Maybe everyone else will leave me too.* Think about those phrases. Are they helpful, or do they set you up for worry, fear or anger? Do they make you feel hopeless and powerless? Do they keep you stuck?

Getting a clear view of your outlook can be painful, so don't allow yourself to wallow. Don't get stuck in the mire of what you've discovered and lapse into self-pity. In the wake of such loss, it's natural to feel pitiful, touchy, angry, or whatever other emotion you experience. But do you want to feel that way forever? If you did, you wouldn't be reading this book. Make a decision to be done now. You're done with the crying, the anger, and the self-pity. You can commit to a change for the better.

STEP TWO: Commit To Positive Change. In Chapter One, you identified what you could not change, and you committed to moving forward for your own good. To accomplish that task, you'll need to recognize the importance of improving your outlook.

Right now, take a few moments to imagine some unknown, uncertain point in the future. See yourself in that future, several months or years from now. I remember wondering: *If my son does return, will he find me wallowing? Fulfilling my own hapless predictions? The woman I'd described on my pitiful list?* **No.** I was determined he would find me well and happy, the capable mother he left.

Even if we never reconciled, imagining myself happy and capable helped me want to reclaim my life—not only for me, but for the people around me whom I love. That tiny glimpse into my imagined future helped me find my way back, and to see myself in a positive light. Strong, resilient, determined. You can do this, too.

Return to the list of adjectives you created in the table in Step One. In the right-hand column, write their opposites. Pick your own words. Here's how part of my list looked:

Negative	Positive: The REAL ME
vulnerable	*resilient*
preoccupied	*present*
stuck	*strong*

Once you have created your second list, give that positive list a title that makes you feel good. For instance, "The Real Me." Or perhaps something like, "The Strong Woman I Am." Then, transfer your titled list of positive words onto a fancy strip of paper, a note card, or your calendar. Put it somewhere handy. On the refrigerator, in your wallet, or tacked to a bulletin board. At one point, I printed words on magnet sheets and stuck them on our exterior doors. That way, I saw the words every time I left the house. If you're into scrapbooking, make a page that features these words, and include a photograph of yourself that you really like. You could also make up a poem with your words, and then sing or say it—*often*. Aim to fulfill the meaning of those positive words.

Now that you've gained more understanding of how negativity may be keeping you down, and have come up with some words to serve as focal points for a fulfilling future, you're ready to move to the last step in powering up a positive outlook.

STEP THREE: Make The Shift. Use your list of positive adjectives to deal with negative thinking and any unhelpful phrases you may speak. Just as it was simple to come up with opposites for the negative words, positive affirmations can spring naturally from negative ones. Review the negative phrases you think or speak often, and then replace them with positive versions. *I'll never get through this*, becomes: *I am moving past this.* If you fear everyone else will leave you too, change it to: *People who love me are in my* *life now.* This positive thought allows you to fully appreciate the people who are with you now, and set aside fears about what they will or won't do. You can't predict the future, but you can enjoy the present.

Now add some positive, forward-thinking statements that increase optimism. Something like: *Good things happen in my life.* Or maybe, *I get through any bad experiences, learn and grow from them. The future is bright.* Use whatever positive statement feels right to you. Just as each of our estrangement situations is unique, we are each individuals with our own set of needs, background and dreams. This is *your* exercise for a positive shift. Embrace it. Add your own spin. Make the positive affirmations your own. Write your positive affirmations here.

_____

_____

_____

_____

_____

_____

_____

_____

_____

_____

_____

_____

_____

_____

_____

_____

_____

_____

_____

_____

_____

_____

Once you're happy with your affirmations, use them as you did with your positive words list. Place your affirmations where you can easily access them. Be creative, or keep it simple. Here are a few ideas: Create a screensaver that scrolls the sayings across your computer screen. Make a bookmark, or post notes on your refrigerator. Create a plaque or a poster. Do what works for *you*. Then use the sayings whenever you catch yourself thinking or saying something that pulls you down. At least a few times, say them aloud, even to the mirror. And say them convincingly. Later, you can think about the affirmations, and remember how emphatically you said them to the mirror earlier.

If this feels strange or doesn't come easily, don't give up. Just like with any kind of exercise, you have to start somewhere. Telling yourself good things may feel odd at first, but commit to doing so every day. That's how habits are formed.

Practice good thinking habits now. Don't wait for negative thoughts to come up before thinking positive ones. When you get up in the morning, make a habit of telling yourself something good. *This will be a good day.* You'll be replacing a bad habit with a good one, which is always helpful. Remember how Julia stopped looking at her cell phone every morning and turned to her list of things-to-do instead? Here, you're similarly substituting a positive action for a negative one. And when you start first thing, you set the tone for your day.

Do as Julia did, and get prepared with ready ways to make your day a good one, so your prediction (*This will be a good day.*) comes true. Make a list of things you can turn to. Do an activity you enjoy. Take a walk outdoors and listen to songbirds. Feel the caress of a gentle breeze. Or notice how sunlight feels against your skin. Even a few moments of delight can break a gloomy mood, and can then be called to mind later and enjoyed again. Call an old friend. Arrange a flower bouquet and put it on your desk at work, or give it to a co-worker. Paint your fingernails to match a holiday or just for fun. Take old bread to a duck pond. Buy a cheesy light-up brooch, and wear it to a meeting or at work. Read a funny novel. Watch a silly YouTube video. Ask a co-worker to take lunch with you in a nearby park. Ride a bicycle up the block. Or bake a cake—whatever you enjoy. Doing even the tiniest activity that once brought you pleasure whets your appetite to do and notice more of what makes you happy, thus shifts your mindset to a new path. Even if you think you don't feel like it, have fun!

Just as negative thoughts of rumination can produce more negativity, positive thoughts can also multiply (and be fruitful). Besides, they feel better, and are good for our health.

- Step One: Gain Awareness.
- Step Two: Commit To Positive Change.
- Step Three: Make The Shift.

Use these three simple steps to power up your positive outlook, cope mindfully in the moment, and live a bright future today.

✈ *Notes*

_____

_____

_____

_____

_____

_____

_____

_____

✈ *Notes*

Get The Support You Need

Support is vital. Chapter Three covers how to go about finding support, whether professional or faith-based, in online groups, or among your friends. Examples and strategies help you devise ready answers for awkward questions and handle situations when you're caught off guard.

✈ Go For a Smart Goal That Supports You

In the midst of any situation in which you feel powerless, it's important to recognize that you *can* do something to help yourself. In fact, there is much you can do to start feeling better. You can begin to support yourself. You can take charge, even incrementally.

The first step is often the biggest, and you've already taken it. For some of you, reading this book was your first step forward. For others, it's one in a series of actions that, even inch-by-inch, are propelling you along on your healing journey. Take another step now. Create a sound goal, and commit to your success. This will begin to help you find solutions. Rather than feeling stuck, you'll begin to train yourself to look for the way forward. You'll begin creating your own supportive path.

Set a goal that helps you find the support you need or assists you in assessing your options for an online or in-person group. Or maybe your goal is to find a good match in a therapist, or make the most of your existing association with a mental health professional. Goals can help you face any estrangement-related issue, and help you create positive change around how it's affecting you.

Maybe you have a goal like Geneva's, which is detailed in *Setting Strong Goals*. Perhaps you need to break a habit that makes you feel bad. That's how Julia stopped reaching for her phone and waiting each morning for the call that wouldn't come. Do you need to reclaim your hobbies, and get back to focusing on things that make you happy? Or do you need to stop looking back, and learn to look forward to your life ahead, no matter how uncertain? A goal can help.

Refer to Geneva's example to see how she clearly defined the intent of her goal, the specific actions she would take to achieve the goal, how she built in a time factor, and measured success. Then use the smart steps below to create and achieve a S.M.A.R.T. goal for your own well-being. Choose one related to finding support, or anything else that's causing you to feel hurt, worry, anger, or any other negativity.

First, reflect on an estrangement-related problem, or a step you'd like to take. Maybe you need to stop looking at Facebook photos that only make you sad. Perhaps you keep asking, "Why?" And you need to focus on a question that better serves you, such as, "What now?"

Remember, goals are about things you can accomplish, not behavior over which you have no control. Make it specific, something you can easily state rather than a big problem with blurry boundaries. As you read through the paragraphs below, you'll work on honing your goal to a fine point that fits all the criteria. Get started now. Write down your basic goal.

_____

_____

_____

_____

Be <u>specific</u>. Now that you've come up with an idea for a goal, let's narrow it down. A goal like, "I want to feel better." is too broad. "I want to look forward to my days again," is an improvement. Still, you can do better. Try: "I want to have a positive focus each and every day."

Look at your goal. Does it clearly and specifically state what you want to achieve? Don't set yourself up for failure. Break a complex goal into smaller goals. Starting small makes it easier to focus and follow through. Success fuels energy for more action, and more success. That's better than setting too many goals at once, and then feeling overwhelmed. Remember, you've been through a horrible trauma. Be kind to yourself. Be your own best friend. Using the example and its improved versions as a guide, expand your goal so it's more specific. Do that now. Write down your expanded goal.

_____

_____

_____

_____

_____

_____

_____

_____

Make it <u>measurable</u>. Our more specific goal, "I want to have a positive focus each and every day," is decent but not so easy to measure. We need some actions associated with the goal. That's how to build in a way to quantify, or otherwise measure your success. Adding some measurable actions, the goal becomes: "*To have a positive focus each day, I'll reflect on an inspirational quote first thing each morning, plus do one special thing just for myself each day.*"

In addition to holding these daily, action-based intentions, a tracking system helps you keep them up. How you track your action can be tailor-made just for you. You could place a checkmark on a calendar, find an accountability partner to whom you routinely report, send yourself a text, or jot a few notes in a journal. This last one helps with self-care ideas too. By recording what you have tried, you can see what worked. What felt right? What was easy on a busy day, and provided a boost, or let you take a breath, feel cared for, and consider what you might need?

While the intent behind the example is to have a more positive focus each and every day, the daily action items provide a structure to move toward the goal. You can also build in more measurability related to a time element. We'll explore that idea more below, in the section on making your goal timely.

Now, look at *your* goal. Have you included measurable actions? Add them now, or make them more concrete. Write down your complete goal.

_____

_____

_____

_____

_____

_____

_____

Aim for the <u>attainable</u>. Analyze your goal. Is it dependent on someone or something else? If so, you'll need to make a change. To succeed, you must be in charge. Consider any factors that might prevent you from taking action. Then, further define or alter the language and focus so you're attempting something you can actually achieve. Just as Geneva's bi-weekly texts conveyed her intended message but did not depend on her daughter's response, your goal must not rely on another's actions.

Let's look at how else the example goal might face obstacles. A quotation book that's pulled off your shelf or purchased specifically for this task is a better option than relying on the dependability of an inspirational email list, or viewing a website that may not be functioning when needed. Such reliance can create barriers that are beyond your control. Goals must rely on you and only you.

We also didn't pinpoint the "one special" thing to be done each day. Set yourself up for success with a ready list of items to do. Making a list precedes attaining the goal. Keep it simple to start. *Enjoy a cup of my favorite tea. Paint my toenails. Sit for 10 minutes by the window and watch the birds. Moisturize my hands with a scented lotion. Trim my fingernails. Chew a stick of gum after lunch. Read the sports page. Watch an uplifting music video. Throw out all my old cosmetics. Enjoy a glass of red wine.* For the example, we would add a few bigger items, too, and take the time to plan them out for easy access and accomplishment. *Get a massage. Take a walk by the river. Spend a weekend away.*

Now, let's get back to *your* goal. On what or whom does your goal rely? Make changes if necessary. Write your goal again. Make note of needed support items. List required telephone numbers, supplies, or whatever else is needed to support your goal.

_____

_____

_____

_____

_____

_____

_____

_____

Keep it <u>realistic</u>. With your available time, knowledge, and resources, do you have the ability to achieve the specified goal? That's a good question to think about and answer. If your goal was to have a positive focus each day, you might keep an inspiring book nearby, and get up earlier to read and reflect. One person might need time to journal about an inspirational quote she's read. Someone else may feel it's sufficient to incorporate reflection into another, perhaps more mindless task (doing dishes, riding the train to work, or taking a shower).

Think through any changes you'll need to make to your schedule. Consider just how the action items you've chosen for your goal will fit into your life. Make a note of these.

_____

_____

_____

_____

_____

Consider the <u>relevance</u>. In addition to standing for "realistic," sometimes, the "R" in S.M.A.R.T. goals is said to stand for "relevant." Because achieving goals takes effort, their *relevance* is important. Take time to consider how useful attaining your goal will be to you. How will this action spur forward momentum, help you reclaim your health and happiness? Knowing this helps you stay motivated and on track. Take a few moments to reflect on the following questions, and then write down your honest and complete answers. Your thoughts get at the "why" behind your goal.

Why is achieving this goal so important to you?

_____

_____

_____

_____

How will achieving this goal affect your life?

_____

_____

_____

_____

Will achieving this goal affect people you care about? How?

_____

_____

_____

_____

Now, using your notes, write out a couple of positive sentences that reinforce your ideas. Craft your thoughts as if they're already achieved. By doing so, you're creating a motivational statement that will help you succeed. A positive motivational statement for our example goal might be:

Purposefully starting my day with a positive focus helps me look forward to my life, keeps me grateful for all the good, and helps me stay hopeful and present for the people I love. Doing something special just for me always makes me feel good, and helps me feel valued. By being my own best friend, I'm better prepared to also be a good friend to those I love.

Write your own motivational statement now. If you feel the need, take time first to ponder this while doing something you enjoy. Then come back feeling refreshed, and write a motivational statement you can believe in. Try a few even, and then settle on one that feels right.

_____

_____

_____

_____

_____

_____

_____

_____

Once you've completed your motivational statement in a way that feels good to you, write it on a notecard and put it where you can easily refer to it for inspiration. Place it where it can remind you daily of the commitment you've made to your goal, and why you feel so strongly.

Keep your goal <u>timely</u>. Our example goal has daily actions, so a time element is built-in. However, there is no set duration for these actions to take place. Adding that element will help with measuring the success of the overall intent (a positive focus each day). Adding a span of time to try the actions associated with carrying out the goal allows for evaluation, changes, and refocusing if needed.

With the example goal, we might evaluate our feelings after one month. We could also track our feelings. In my writing work for a nonprofit organization helping those with depression, I assisted in creating a monitoring kit for people to track their emotions. Two or three times a day, they could draw a happy or sad face, or write down a word or two to describe their feelings. Used along with a journal, they could then associate their emotions with what was going on in their lives.

For our example goal, using the awareness gained by doing the exercise, *Power Up A Positive Outlook*, at the end of Chapter Two will help. You could also reflect on your feelings at the end of each day or week, and then evaluate your overall outlook at the end of the month.

Whatever your goal is, factoring in a deadline or other time-related measurement is important. These sorts of questions apply: *By what date will you achieve your goal? For how many days/weeks will you continue before evaluating your success? On which days of the week will you do the goal-oriented actions?* Jot down your answers now.

_____

_____

_____

_____

Goals are transformative. Even when we craft our goals and create action steps to achieve them and to stay on track, heartaches, stress, and obstacles can slap us back. Staying motivated is a challenge. So, in my work as a life coach, I crafted another S.M.A.R.T. acronym that focuses on the prize: **_Stay Motivated And Realize Transformation._**

During my darkest hours, to **_Stay Motivated And Realize Transformation_**, sprang to mind, a beacon. It helped me put the experience in perspective and recognize the heartrending situation of my son's estrangement for what it was: an unexpected turn. While my life had changed, it wasn't over. I had overcome obstacles in the past. I had lived through horrendous experiences before—and I would live through this too. In fact, the hurt and loss provided me an opportunity to step forward, and prove again what I have witnessed in my own and others' lives: *The landscape of loss is fertile ground for growth.*

That realization helped me to accept my son's choices, and move forward with decisions for my own well-being. I could get on with the work of setting and achieving goals to rebuild my outlook and my life. In the aftermath of emotional devastation, I could search for building blocks to create an even better life and a more fully realized me. *And so can you.*

✈ At Your Best

Reflect on how you've successfully dealt with problems in the past. Reliving those satisfying moments can break a habit of self-blame or self-pity, and trigger more positive feelings about the future. In fact, writing about a time when you were at your best, and then reflecting on the memory daily for a week, has been shown to increase well-being.

After reading through the next few paragraphs, use the lines to describe you at your very best. Perhaps you are a sunny person, even in times of trouble. Or you prioritize what's important, and focus on the present moment. Maybe you are caring and careful of how your speech and actions affect others. Maybe people or pets are drawn to you. Maybe you can make anything grow, and see things from every possible side.

In your written description, remember a time when you were at your best, or create a story in which you use your strengths. Perhaps imagine you're stranded on an island. You don't waste a moment crying. You befriend island natives, wow them with magic tricks, and gain their trust. Your attention to detail allows you to quickly learn their survival skills, and you lead the stranded group off the island without a hitch.

In my work as a life coach, some clients wrote poems to describe themselves at their best. Others made up songs, hymns, or created a simple list. Descriptions ran the gamut. The exercise works well when you do what feels right to you.

Describing yourself at your best, in writing, can reconnect you with your values, your strengths, and your accomplishments, and provide you with bolstering words that you can read through on another day. Remembering who you are at your best will boost your self-respect, and spur your interest and energy into activities you enjoy and do well.

Me at my best: _____

_____

_____

_____

_____

_____

_____

_____

_____

_____

_____

_____

_____

_____

_____

The next logical step is to think about using your best self to conquer the heartache and prevail in your life. Reflect on what you've written about yourself.

Now, concentrating on your strengths, imagine a year has passed. Enter the future now, imagine your best self, and describe what you see. What are you doing with yourself and your life? Are you happy? Have you moved ahead? Do you feel free? Write about it now.

One year from now—me at my best: _____

_____

_____

_____

_____

_____

_____

✈ *Notes*

CHAPTER FOUR

Ready, Set, Prepare

Useful strategies help you maintain your dignity and self-respect. You can anticipate *damned-if-you-do* and *damned-if-you-don't* scenarios, and cope in ways that honor your values and keep you feeling strong.

✈ Take Stock

Take a few moments (or even a few days), to consider how the estrangement has affected you—your life, your relationships, your mood, your habits. Use the space in the boxes here to consider the effects in writing. Your notes will be useful as you continue forward. Taking the time to examine what's going on in your life will provide awareness (knowledge) and insight that can help you take positive action (power). For now, simply take stock of the effects by recording them. Don't worry about getting too meticulous, but be as detailed as feels right. You're becoming more aware, and forming a solid foundation for positive action toward solutions.

Let's Begin. Use the categories listed to reflect on your life since your child has been estranged. *How do you feel? What is missing? What are you doing well? How can you improve?* The headings are in no particular order. If one area feels easier than another, feel free to work in the order that best suits you. Be honest. Don't censor yourself.

Avoid the urge to answer as you would have before the estrangement, or how you'd like to be. Your candid reflections help you examine your life as it stands right now. Later, your notes will help you create achievable goals to move forward. For now, quickly jot down ideas that might be of help to you.

At the beginning, I've placed an optional section where you can add an additional area you choose, such as your physical environment or career.

Optional: *Add an area you define.*

Emotional Well-Being/Happiness: *How has the estrangement affected your attitude and happiness?*

What can you do to feel better?

Health & Fitness: *Since the estrangement began, has your health & fitness level declined? How?*

In what ways can you take better care of yourself?

Friends, Family and Social Connection: *Since the estrangement, have you neglected, lost, or maintained relationships and social commitments?*

How can you improve in this area?

Personal Growth/Dreams: *Since the estrangement, have you given up something important to you? How has the estrangement affected your outlook?*

How can you begin to make changes for the better?

Leisure & Fun: *Since the estrangement, do you still have fun and enjoy leisure time?*

How can you do more to enjoy yourself?

Money & Wealth: *Since the estrangement, do you spend more (or less)? Have your thoughts or feelings about money and finances changed?*

How might you do and feel better in this area?

Significant Other/Love Relationship: *How has your relationship changed since the estrangement? What are your worries?*

How can this area be improved? What would make things better?

Spirituality/Fulfillment: *How has your spirituality and/or sense of fulfillment changed since the estrangement?*

How might you feel more spiritually fulfilled?

Self-Image/Self-Esteem: *Since the estrangement, has your self-esteem/self-image changed? What is different? Why?*

What can you do to feel better about yourself?

The *Take Stock* exercise is intended to create a foundation for you to build upon later. We'll return to your notes in Chapter Nine.

✈ Visualize Your Child's Happy Life

Though angry and hurt, thousands of parents share the hope that the children they nurtured will do well. This loving thought that's so common among supportive parents can be put to good use for themselves. To free yourself, adapt, and embrace your future, wish your child well. Visualize your child happy, healthy, and living a meaningful life.

Before Starting: Keep in mind that if you are forever checking in on your child through Facebook or other social networks, this exercise may not be successful. Seeing details in online photos can upset you. If your son has lost weight, you may worry about his health. If beer bottles cluster on a table behind your daughter, you may fear she's drinking too much. Speculation can be endless, and defeats the purpose of this exercise. Honor your adult child's wishes to separate from you. *For your own good*, stop lurking in his or her life.

Be aware that the positive results of this exercise are for *you*. Your thoughts don't have an effect on your child's life, and don't magically fix your relationship with him or her. The results follow the spirit of this book: acceptance, and moving successfully forward in your own life. By wishing your child well, despite his choices or whether or not her path leads back to you, you set the stage to let go of worry, anger, pride, or expectation. You set *yourself* free to embrace the present.

Let's Begin: Choose a quiet space: in your bedroom with the lights dimmed, in a comfortable outdoor setting, or as you close your eyes before falling asleep. Then, using the tips below, visualize your child as happy, well-adjusted, loved, and content.

TIPS FOR SUCCESS

- **Resist the urge to overthink details.** If your child dreamed of becoming a doctor but quit school and rejected you, don't create a detailed drama that chronicles her recapturing that goal. This isn't about specifics that feed abandoned expectations or fulfill your hopes. Don't visualize detailed scenarios that set you up for further disappointment. Imagine your child happy and satisfied, period.

- **Frame this visualization to fit your beliefs.** My first iteration of this exercise was a prayer. A peaceful visual of my son and his life in a loving Creator's hands. A blessing of sorts. If using your belief system feels right to you, then utilize that to provide some structure. Or simply imagine without any specific beliefs in mind. Visualize your child as a kind adult, engaged in meaningful activities such as caring for animals, playing music, or cooking.

- **Repeat this exercise and allow it to evolve.** My initial prayer progressed into helpful snapshots, fleeting but intentional imaginings like my son walking out a door, golden sunlight shining on his path. Create and recreate this simple exercise. Turn to it when you're worried or you long for the child you so miss. Use positive visualization whenever needed, in a brief yet meaningful way that lets you let go.

- **Remember, this is not an exercise to control results in your child's life.** Visualizing your child well and happy will help *you*.

- **If it feels right for you, use your physical body to support this exercise.** Open your hands, and imagine letting tension go, and also releasing your child. Do what works for you. Close your eyes, open your palms to the sky, or assume a meditational pose. Make this exercise yours.

- **Add powerful thoughts and images to support you.** Breathe deeply. Imagine inhaling peace, confidence, and love. When you exhale, visualize worry, anger, and all negativity swirling out and away from you.

- **Make it real.** Picture your son's laughing eyes. See your daughter's flawless skin or shining hair. Imagine welcoming faces, a table spread with healthy foods, a cozy living space, and a life full of hugs and joy. . . . Create imagery that feels good and makes you smile. Whether you're ever part of that wonderful life, want that for your child. Believe in it.

As you heal from the harrowing pain of estrangement, you may find, as I did, that these positive visualizations become briefer, but also more fulfilling: a fleeting picture you can conjure up at any time to strengthen you; an image that helps you to trust that all will be well. And then you can turn to your own life, your own sunlit path.

✈ *Notes*

✈ *Notes*

CHAPTER FIVE

See Your Feelings In a New Light

Gaping holes require patching, and you've already begun the process. Give yourself credit for how much you've grown. Loads of specific strategies exemplified by smart parents, help you come to terms with uncomfortable feelings (anger, guilt, bitterness, and rage, to name a few). Letting go does not mean giving up. *You're not a quitter. You're a starter—in a new phase of life!*

✈ *Help Wanted?* **Help Yourself**

What's Missing? Start with a list of the roles your estranged son or daughter fulfilled. These can be practical things like cook, gardener, and computer assistant. Or less tangible roles, like the person who filled the house with live music, or lifted the atmosphere with all their friends.

Roles Your Child Filled:	Making Up For The Loss:

Once you've made your list, take note of which activities you now do for yourself—and feel proud. Or, if you've sought outside assistance, grown in some way as an individual or as a family, give yourself credit for the change. While loss hurts, there's also a positive side. It provides room to grow, and teaches us new things.

If you can't think of many things you now do for yourself, don't worry. Identifying where you can make positive changes is helpful. We'll deal with filling those roles in a moment.

Give yourself some love. Now, come up with a few statements to explain the growth. Even if you can only think of one small thing, give yourself credit. You've adapted to change! Here are some examples:

- I have the patience and intelligence to learn how technology works, and can set most of it up. Because of this, I'm more independent. It feels good to know that I can adapt to change.

- I now know that I can look for, and even hire help. Hired help, in fact, is more prompt, dependable, and takes less time.

- I have learned to ask friends for help. There is always someone who *wants* to help. People enjoy being needed.

- I've learned more about letting go, realizing that even if I do my best, some things are beyond my control. This has helped me worry less about outcomes, and enjoy the present more.

Now, write down a few positive statements of your own about how you have grown, adapted, or positively changed.

_____

_____

_____

_____

_____

_____

_____

_____

_____

Fill in the blanks. Some of your child's roles will remain empty. Notice them. They're part of the loss. Think of ways to fulfill the roles not yet occupied. If you enjoyed that your child played music, you can buy show tickets, attend free concerts, play CDs, or learn an instrument yourself. If you haven't already done so, go back to your list of roles, and fill in how they're being filled, or ways you might fill them.

Shift perspective, and acknowledge positives. What *don't* you miss? Be honest. If your son or daughter always had friends over, you may now enjoy the quiet. Did your child often initiate deep discussions that you weren't ready for, or that became combative or frustrating? Was your child verbally abusive? It's fair to admit you don't miss the ugly words or the arguments.

Right now, think of a few things that you *don't* miss. Do you have more space, more time, or more money? Is there less overall strife, or are there fewer distractions? Are you glad you aren't put on the spot? Called to be available when you already have plans? Perhaps you're relieved not to walk on egg-shells around your child's unkind spouse. Although born of heartache, it's okay to recognize that some things are better. There's no need to feel guilty for those feelings.

_____

_____

_____

_____

_____

_____

_____

_____

Estrangement is a force you must reckon with. Just as you have done with other losses you've experienced in life, you can learn and grow. You can choose to live a happy and fulfilling life. Look at the lists you've created here. You can get past this. In some ways, you already have.

✈ The Good Life: Yours

In Chapter Four, we explored the idea of wishing our children well. We visualized him or her in a happy life. We reflected on what that would look like and mean, and saw our children successful, well, and content. In order to adapt and embrace our own future, now let's turn to our own sunlit path. Visualize yourself happy, healthy, and living a meaningful life.

Before Starting: You may want to look at your notes from the *Take Stock* exercise in Chapter Four. Doing so will provide insight into how you've changed since the estrangement, and enable you to see yourself on-the-mend, fortifying deficits, and getting back in touch with yourself, your dreams, the activities you enjoy, and the people who are important to you.

The positive results of this exercise are for *you.* Your wishes cannot magically fix your child's life or your relationship with him or her. Please make this about your life, separate and apart from any possible relationship with your child now or in the future. Imagining what a satisfying life looks like on your own, and perhaps with others who choose to be with you, follows the spirit of this book: acceptance, and moving successfully forward in your own life. Earlier, you wished your child well. Now wish yourself well. By letting go of trying to control another person's choices, or making your happiness dependent on what they may or may not do, you strengthen yourself. You set the stage to let go of worry, anger, pride, or expectation. You set yourself free to embrace the present.

Let's Begin: Choose a quiet space such as in your bedroom with the lights dimmed, or in a comfortable outdoor setting. Or you could try this as you close your eyes before falling asleep at night. Using the tips, visualize yourself as happy, well-adjusted, loved, and content. What does that look like to you?

TIPS FOR SUCCESS

- Resist the urge to overthink details. This isn't about detailed scenarios. We're going for impressions here. Blissful images, wishes, and dreams.

- Allow thoughts and images to drift in, and then analyze how you feel about them. If something causes tension, makes you angry or sad, direct yourself to let the image go. Then refocus with a clear intent. Ask yourself: *What makes me feel happy?* Do you see yourself all smiles, sharing time with your partner? Are you outdoors? Successful and engaged at work? Walking along the shore? Imagine yourself in the scene.

- Frame this visualization to fit your beliefs. Perhaps you say a prayer. Maybe you imagine yourself in a loving Creator's hands, or ask for a blessing. Or simply imagine without any specific beliefs in mind. Visualize yourself as contented and engaged in meaningful tasks.

- If it feels right, include your physical body too. Close your eyes, open your palms to the sky, or assume a meditational pose.

- Use your breath. Add powerful thoughts and images to support you. Imagine inhaling peace, confidence, and love. When you exhale, visualize worry, anger, and all negativity swirling out and away from you.

- If words or phrases come to you, let them. For me, the phrase "dancing through life," was immediately prominent. The words felt good, and allowed positive imagery to fall into my mind and heart. Whatever dark clouds or full-on storms came my way, I could weather them. I could still feel joy, see the good, and cherish the beautiful—I could dance through life.

Make It Tangible: Now that you've imagined yourself happy, contented, and moving on with your life, make it real. Using a computer program or magazine cut outs, make a collage. Or draw what your visualization looks like. My creation depicted me (as a clip art figure, much like a child). I danced along a path lined with wildflowers and other items I love. The words "dancing through life," are prominent. So is sunlight, and spiritual imagery—to provide me with energy and strength.

Six months after my son first became estranged I printed out and shared my creation with friends as part of a goal-setting meeting. If it helps you, then share your creation with people you trust to support you. You might also hang it in a place you'll see it often. If you tuck it away in a drawer or some other safe, *out-of-sight* place, don't let it also be *out-of-mind*. Pull it out now and again, and allow the imagery to strengthen your beliefs. You can be happy. You can be whole. *You can be dancing through life.*

Make It Tangible: Drawing Space

Make It Tangible: Drawing Space

✈ *Notes*

CHAPTER SIX

Managing Effects On The Family

Estrangement affects the whole family. Learn to navigate the murky waters of parenting other children, communicating about the missing sibling, and more. Marriage partners can communicate better and work out any issues of blame. Use the M.O.M. acronym to break free of fear, live in the present, and protect yourself and your family.

✈ Affirmative Statements

Revisit the affirmative statements you created in Chapter Two's *Power a Positive Outlook* exercise. Mine went like this: *I am a strong woman and a good mother. My value is not tied up with or diminished by my son's rejection. His decision has more to do with him than me, even if I don't understand it. Neither does his behavior predict my other children's.*

Can you come to similar conclusions? Use the ones you came up with earlier, or write down some positive thoughts about yourself now.

_____

_____

_____

_____

_____

_____

_____

_____

_____

_____

_____

_____

_____

✈ The Shape of Your Family

Refer to the opening of this chapter where we talked of the family as a shape or form. Maybe your estranged child made up a family of three, forming a triangle as in Pauline and her husband's case. Remove one, and your triangle breaks. Two lines connect at a single point. Pauline has grown stronger through all of this. She's straightened her shoulders and stood up tall. Instead of broken triangle parts, maybe now she thinks of herself and her husband as two pillars, side-by-side, but each complete.

If you think of your family as a square, when one section walks away the others can bend and curve to make a circle instead. A family that joins hands in a circle, but now has an estranged and missing piece, can choose to draw in closer—or perhaps open wide for new relationships.

In your mind, or with paper and pen, play with ideas to fix your triangle, join your circle, become a new and even stronger shape. Don't settle for a broken triangle. You *can* close the gap, assess and reshape, and develop into a new and even better form.

In the alternative, conjure up an imaginative symbol for your family. In a creative writing class years ago, students were required to choose and write about a metaphor to represent their families. I chose a forest, where trees stand uniquely strong, yet together form a safe, inviting place. Sunlight penetrates for swaths of warmth, yet restful shade persists. Even without Dan, I see my family as a lovely forest. The image still comforts me.

Come up with positive imagery for your post-estrangement family. Draw a picture, paint one with words, paste magazine cut-outs, or simply let your imagination soar. Use the space here and on the next page if you'd like to.

Remember, it's only an idea, a snapshot in time. If your child someday returns in a way that suits you, the picture can be changed. If the idea doesn't feel right to you tomorrow, you can flex and bend. It's *your* imagination. Make it work for you.

The Shape of Your Family: Drawing Space

The Shape of Your Family: Drawing Space

CHAPTER SEVEN

What Does It Mean To Reconcile?

Parents must come to terms with what has occurred, alter quixotic hopes, and see reconciliation from a realistic perspective. Take charge. You have a right to do what's best for you and your family in the present. The ghosts of hope, love, and pain may come to visit, but you don't have to let them stay. Without glasses tinted a rosy hue from past happiness or wishful thinking, you define your future with a clear-eyed view.

✈ Examine Your Relationship

Healthy adult relationships require boundaries and mutual respect. Is that the sort of relationship you have shared with your estranged child? Often, estranged parents find themselves pining for the sweet child they once knew, or getting caught up in old expectations. Let's take a realistic look. Reflect on the questions. In your answers, elaborate in order to think the questions through.

- Was the relationship one-sided? *How?* Did I allow my adult child to manipulate or take advantage of me? *How?*

_____

_____

_____

_____

_____

_____

- Did my child cut me off when I drew boundaries, stood up for myself, required her to contribute, or to pay his own way? How?

_____

_____

_____

_____

_____

_____

- Was my child physically or emotionally abusive, or disrespectful to me? How? When?

_____

_____

_____

_____

_____

_____

_____

_____

- Did I dread visits? Was I often inconvenienced, or feel used? When?

_____

_____

_____

_____

_____

_____

_____

_____

- Was I reminded of "mistakes," or made to feel guilty? List examples.

_____

_____

_____

_____

_____

_____

_____

_____

- Did our interactions often make me angry or resentful? How/Why?

_____

_____

_____

_____

_____

_____

_____

_____

- Did I feel the need to be careful what I said or did? If so, how?

_____

_____

_____

_____

_____

_____

_____

_____

Look back on what you've written. For a few minutes, allow yourself to reflect on the relationship. Remember incidents, recall your feelings, and take notice of how the memories manifest in your physical body.

- Do I want to go back to that same sort of relationship? Write down your thoughts/emotions.

_____

_____

_____

_____

_____

_____

_____

_____

Sharing with a counselor, a trusted friend, or in a support group might be helpful, but that's for you to decide—later. Don't censor yourself here. Your thoughts and feelings are valid, and worthy of your attention.

If an inequitable, unkind, or hurtful relationship feels necessary, or appeals to you more than honoring your values and what you know is healthy for you, take an honest look at what's behind that notion. When you ask yourself *why* you are willing to dishonor yourself—your health, your happiness, your financial wellbeing, or in any other way—what thoughts and feelings occur to you?

_____

_____

_____

_____

_____

_____

_____

_____

_____

_____

If, after doing the exercise, you feel that *any* relationship with an adult son or daughter, even one in which you feel used or abused, is more desirable than *no* relationship or perhaps a very limited one, it's important that you consider what might be behind those feelings. As an example, co-dependency could be a factor. It's equally possible that you suffer low self-esteem, or perhaps your natural temperament is one that avoids conflict (even to your own peril).

The thrust of this book is reclaiming your life. Self-reflection can be a part of that.

✈ Reconciling: What It Means, What It Takes

With the above examples and your own situation, in mind, ponder the questions. Write down your thoughts, feelings, and answers. Don't censor yourself.

• What does reconciliation mean to me?

_____

_____

_____

_____

_____

_____

_____

• Is my view of reconciliation currently possible? Why/Why not?

_____

_____

_____

_____

_____

_____

_____

- Am I willing to compromise or alter my thoughts about what it means to reconcile? How?

_____

_____

_____

_____

_____

_____

_____

- Realistically, what would I have to do to reconcile at this time? Would the reconciliation be real?

_____

_____

_____

_____

_____

_____

_____

_____

- How would I have to adjust my thinking, actions, and beliefs?

_____

_____

_____

_____

_____

_____

_____

_____

- What am I willing to do to reconcile?

_____

_____

_____

_____

_____

_____

_____

_____

- What would my child have to do for me to believe the reconciliation was genuine?

_____

_____

_____

_____

_____

_____

_____

_____

_____

- Knowing that a decision I make today does not have to forever bind me, can I "reconcile to the facts," as was discussed in this chapter?

_____

_____

_____

_____

CHAPTER EIGHT

Life Goes On

For many parents, estrangements take place simultaneously with other disruptive transitions that can pile on stress. Topics include grandparents' rights, estate planning, and other "time of life" matters. With a positive attitude, healthful strategies, support from provided resources, and real-life examples, you can prevail.

✈ Decisions for My Estate: Questions to Help

- Do I want my estranged child to benefit from my estate?

_____

_____

_____

- Will I provide for my estranged child's children?

_____

_____

_____

- How will my other beneficiaries be impacted by including my estranged child?

_____

_____

_____

- Are my other children/beneficiaries in contact with my estranged child?

_____

_____

_____

- Is my estranged child likely to cause issues for other beneficiaries?

_____

_____

_____

✈ Nearing the End of Life: Will Your Adult Child Be Informed?

We all know that at some point our physical lives here on Earth will end. While you may have always assumed your children would be near, a child's estrangement adds uncertainty. This can be an uncomfortable topic, but it's something you need to think about. Contemplating your final days can help you make important decisions.

The visualization and questions below are designed to help you clarify your feelings, anticipate potential problems, and make a plan that provides you with peace of mind. Start with this question: *If you faced a terminal condition, would you want someone else deciding whether or not your estranged child should be informed?*

_____

_____

Imagine lying in a hospital bed, knowing you are soon to die. Imagine the people you *know* will be at your side. See them there with you. Reflect upon their feelings and your own. Then imagine your estranged adult child entering the room.

• *How does the scene unfold? Who else is present? How do they react? Does arguing occur? Do peole hug?*

_____

_____

_____

_____

_____

_____

_____

_____

Picture the scene. Fully imagine how you will feel as the interactions take place. As you contemplate the situation, reflect on any thoughts that come to mind: possible problems, whether or not you can control what's happening, and worries over how you and anyone else present will feel or respond.

Now, with all of this in mind, ask yourself: *Do I want my estranged child present?*

If so, or if you're still uncertain, consider these questions:

- *How can you work* now *to minimize potential problems?*

_____

_____

_____

_____

_____

_____

- *What can you do to prepare loved ones in advance?*

_____

_____

_____

_____

_____

_____

_____

You could talk to your loved ones in advance, and maybe even ask for their input. Then, with a clear picture formed by your own desires and others' responses, you can make a plan.

If you decide that you want your estranged son or daughter informed, you'll need to choose someone to perform the task. Also choose an alternate person as a backup. *Who do you feel can best handle the task?*

If another of your children may be angry at the estranged child, he or she may not be the right choice. Choose those who are level-headed and able to keep their emotions in check.

- *In your life, who is best suited?*

_____

_____

_____

Really consider who might best handle the task. Be sure to talk with these people about the role you'd like to assign them. Your plan won't work if someone is taken by surprise and refuses to make the call.

Also, consider parameters. A variety of scenarios might occur, so consider in what situations your estranged child should be informed.

- *Do you want your estranged son called only in the event you are placed in hospice care and your remaining time is limited?*

_____

_____

_____

- *Shall your estranged daughter be informed if you are terminally ill, but are still at home living independently?*

_____

_____

_____

- *What if injury causes a coma or you're on life support? Then should your estranged child be called?*

_____

_____

_____

You might also imagine how the conversation will go.

- *What might your estranged son or daughter ask or say?*

_____

_____

_____

_____

_____

_____

_____

_____

_____

_____

_____

_____

_____

- *What if she asks whether you want her to come? How do you want your representative to respond?*

_____

_____

_____

_____

_____

_____

_____

_____

_____

_____

_____

_____

_____

_____

_____

_____

_____

Taking account of all of your thoughts and responses, write out a plan. Provide specific instructions. The more you have reflected on your feelings, the more direction you'll be prepared to give. Thus, the person you've chosen to make the contact will feel secure and confident in completing the task. Perhaps you will write a short script, so your designated caller can rely upon it—even telling your estranged son or daughter they are reading a script provided by you.

No matter what you decide, no one will know your requests unless you tell them. Apprise the people who will be charged with the task of honoring your wishes.

_____

_____

_____

_____

_____

_____

_____

_____

_____

_____

_____

_____

_____

_____

CHAPTER NINE

Walk Forward

There is wisdom in knowing when it's time to "fold," letting go of sorrows and expectations in favor of moving ahead and finding meaning in everyday life. Learn from your own past patterns of strength and savor your positive experiences. Pull out the image you created in the *Make It Tangible* part of the *Visualize Your Life* exercise from Chapter Five. *See yourself in that beautiful light.*

✈ Who Are You Really? What's Your Mission?

Who are you? What's in your heart? Compose a statement for yourself, a mission of sorts, in its simplest, truest form. Don't overthink or struggle with this idea. This isn't about creating a "mission statement" as the term is known in business. There's no requirement to answer specific questions as they apply to specific goals. It's more about your essence as a human being, as in the example: *I'm a kind person who cares about and nurtures myself and others.* It's a statement of belief that provides focus. Something you can remind yourself of as you wake each morning, or at times when you're feeling stressed, frustrated, or even defeated. Here are a few more examples:

- I live a life of prayer, which helps me demonstrate grace to myself and others.

- I notice what others miss or what doesn't get done, so I often pick up the slack. It feels good to help.

- I am a good listener, and because of that, have insights to share.

- Even in the tensest moments, I find what's funny. I make people laugh.

Your answers in Chapter Three's *At Your Best* exercise can help you identify what invigorates you, or where your passions lie. If you need to, remember what you were like pre-estrangement. Search your heart for positive answers. Would you call yourself ordered? Do you thrive on routine? Do you defer to a higher power? Are you innovative? Are you at your best when you're helping other people? Maybe you look for and find the good in every situation. Perhaps your highest value is inner peace, and you make a point of conducting yourself to foster that feeling. Have people always gravitated to your high energy, your sense of humor, or your natural ability to lead? Perhaps they come to you when they're feeling low because your presence is naturally calming.

How do you define yourself? Phrasing such as, "I lift people's spirits," and "I'm an encourager," can boost self-esteem. Or, something like, "I provide a calming presence," can help make your own mood serene. "I make people laugh," can help you find the humor in day-to-day life—and share it. Your unique sensibilities, shared, might make someone's day (or your own!).

Think of and write out a statement or two that reinforce these ideas. Transfer your words about yourself to the bulletin board, or write them on pretty note paper and put them in a convenient spot. Read them each morning, and then set about your simple mission every day.

_____

_____

_____

_____

_____

✦ Be Resilient

Loosely defined as thriving despite adversity, resilience is enhanced by context, outlook, mastery, and enjoyment.

How can you enhance your own resilience, despite the loss? Search your memory for adversity you've overcome. Resilient people draw on past experiences as far back as childhood to help them deal with current hardship. They have been through difficulties before, and are confident they will again prevail.

In a 2008 study, the most resilient older adults discussed sorrows and misfortunes in a whole-life context, and in the past tense. Talking about all of the things they'd been through helped the participants to see themselves as surviving those stressors, and going on to thrive. The patterns they found centered on how they had coped and continued on. We can learn from their resilience.

Recall some traumatic events of your life. Reach back as far as you'd like, or choose more recent events. It's not necessary to choose your absolute worst traumas. Think or write about a remembered event or two in the past tense. How did you cope? If you can, identify patterns in how you managed the stress and moved beyond it. Did you turn to close friends or family to encourage you? Did you use your sorrow to spur you forward, pursue education, or a dream? Perhaps you learned to ask for help, grew closer to God, or learned how strong you could be.

_____

_____

_____

_____

_____

_____

_____

_____

_____

_____

Now that you've identified past experiences you can you draw strength and learn from, apply the knowledge to your current situation. You have successfully moved forward before. Be confident in the reality that you're even wiser now.

What's your story? How have you coped in the past? How can you apply your own unique sensibilities to moving past your current pain?

_____

_____

_____

_____

_____

_____

_____

_____

_____

_____

_____

_____

_____

_____

_____

Rowena pulled herself out of the doldrums by remembering her mother's strength.

"I cried for weeks," she says. "People do cry when bad things happen. But eventually, I dried my tears and got on with life. Getting on with life is what we strong women do."

Connecting her predicament to her mother's strength, and the strength of *all* women, reminded Rowena of her own strength. As always, she would "get on with life." That sort of coping is a resilient pattern in her life.

How can your life experiences help you to reclaim your identity or devise a stronger one?

Recall the simple mission statement(s) you created in the last exercise. In the next set of lines, try formulating a phrase or two that propel you forward, such as Rowena's belief that she always gets on with her life. Or my frequent saying, based on past struggles I've survived: *Everything will be okay.* Do that now.

_____

_____

_____

_____

_____

_____

_____

_____

_____

_____

✈ Take Notice, And Savor

The best things in life may be free, but not unless we take notice and appreciate them. Let's take a closer look at savoring—in the moment, in memory, in anticipating—and what it can do for you.

Feeling satisfaction or pride, and holding positive beliefs about your work or a hobby can be considered savoring. As can enjoying anything in the moment, and then remembering it later, or looking forward to being immersed in it again. These sorts of positive feelings and beliefs about one's activities, *savoring*, foster resilience, and lend meaning to life.

What do you find enchanting? What takes your breath away, makes time pass without awareness, and allows you to simply be? Right now, think of at least three pastimes that bring you joy. As you list them, take a moment to savor your positive experiences.

_____

_____

_____

Then write down three more things to try, that will bring you joy.

_____

_____

_____

Think about making more time for all of these things, and anticipate the possible feelings you'll derive: *elation, pride, connection, freedom, joy.* Come up with some positive feeling words of your own. Write them down, and say them aloud. Get used to using those feel-good words. Use them often to describe and savor your experiences.

_____

_____

_____

You may already practice more savoring than you realize. Do you ever hit the pillow at night, and find yourself smiling about something somebody said that day? That's savoring, and it feels great. Make a game of finding things to savor. During almost any activity, if you're *looking* for things to later savor your whole outlook changes for the better.

✈ Practical Steps for Your Bright Future

Look back at your answers in the Chapter Four exercise, *Take Stock*. You took a hard look at how much you've changed since the estrangement began. Now, do something useful with that knowledge. Give it power.

What areas do you need most to improve in? Perhaps your sadness and preoccupation have taken a toll on family relationships, and you know you need to spend time and energy with the people you love. Or maybe you have a tendency to shop when you're feeling low, so recognize a need to better budget, and to get your financial life in order. Is your spiritual health calling for attention? Or does the *Take Stock* exercise show you that your mood crept into your leisure time, so that you no longer make room for recreation and fun. Maybe you've neglected important friendships. You've worked at restoring yourself. Now, expand the healing into all areas of your life.

Choose two areas where you can improve. You can use the S.M.A.R.T. goals method to devise plans to make progress. Or simply start by identifying two or three small things you can take action on within the next few days. Write your action items down. Then do them.

Let's look at a couple of examples.

If you chose to focus on your finances, you might begin with the following steps:

1. skip buying your morning Latte, and brew coffee at home instead

2. pay for everything with cash, and then save the change for a specific purpose

3. create a food budget and shop with a list

For better health, three action steps might be:

1. try a new vegetable

2. walk around the block on your lunch hour

3. swear off fast food for a month

You decide. Make your steps meaningful, but choose things you know you can accomplish. Give yourself a challenge, but don't make the tasks too daunting. Success builds confidence. When you feel better about the two areas in which you've chosen to work, reevaluate, and make more changes as needed. Then choose two more. Your goals can get bigger as you progress. Working on specific areas helps you move forward with purpose as you reclaim your happy, meaningful life.

Mark your calendar to do the *Take Stock* exercise again in two to three months, and see how you've improved. Celebrate your success. *You're not running a race. You're stepping forward—or even dancing through life.*

✈ *Notes*

✈ Notes

✈ *Notes*

✈ Notes

✈ *Notes*

✈ Notes

✈ *Notes*

✈ *Notes*

✈ *Notes*

✈ Notes

✈ Notes

ABOUT THE AUTHOR

Sheri McGregor holds a bachelor's degree in psychology, a master's degree in human behavior, and is a certified life coach. She has served on the advisory board for National University's College of Letters and Sciences.

In her writing career of more than two decades, McGregor's articles on psychology, health, and a variety of other topics have appeared in dozens of national and international publications. She has also written for anthologies, websites, and organizations including the non-profit Families for Depression Awareness. In her three hiking guides, McGregor leads readers down the trails with descriptions that reveal her appreciation for nature and how it calms the mind.

Her work to help parents of estranged adult children began at RejectedParents.NET, which she founded in late 2013. You can sign up for her email newsletter at the site. She also maintains a Facebook page, located at facebook.com/rejectedparents. As a caring mother to whom the unthinkable happened, Sheri McGregor has become a powerful voice for the parents of estranged adult children.

Made in the USA
Coppell, TX
03 September 2020